To

Luke

Chin Chin

St. T

30/9/14

Robber

photographs by
Steven Tynan

First published in 1995 by
Robber Books
8 Claremont Road
Teddington
Middlessex TW11 8DG
Telephone: 0181 943 1613
Facsimile: 0181 943 4446

Edition 1000 casebound

ISBN 0 9526728 0 4

© Robber Books, Steven Tynan, Sylvia Grant
and Paul Caplin

British Library Cataloguing in Publication
Data. A catalogue record for this book is
available from the British Library

FOR MY MUM AND DAD,
ALL MY LOVE

Design: Alan Ward @ Axis, Manchester
0161 882 0004

Robber is distributed by:
Cornerhouse Publications
70 Oxford Street
Manchester
M1 5NH
Telephone 0161 237 9662
Facsimile 0161 237 9664

LET'S START WITH A HAPPINESS, WHAT'S MONEY HONEY? WEALTH CAN BE IN WALKING, TO BE OUTSIDE. SHE TAKES A WALK AROUND THE HORSESHOE OF COMMON LAND THAT COMES DOWN FROM THE MOORS.

SOME DAYS ARE LIKE THIS, CLOUDLESS. WHAT CLOUDS THERE ARE, INTERNAL. THE CATARACTS OF EXPERIENCE, WORRY, LEARNING, CARRIED AROUND TO SOMETIMES MASK THIS CLEAR VISION OF A DAY.

HERE IS A PHOTOGRAPH. IN FURS, UP-FRONT, FIERCE PERHAPS. I LIKE TO LOOK WITH IT, READY.

WHAT IS IT HERE TO BE OF AN AGE? STANDING NOW BEFORE CURTAINS, BEHIND CLOSED DOORS IN THE CAMOUFLAGE OF ARTIFICIAL LIGHT, NOT AN EXILE IN A NEW LAND BUT TO BE A PRUDENT PIONEER IN UNEVEN LANDSCAPES WHERE OFTEN A STICK IS REQUIRED.

TO REST IN ROOMS WITH CUSHIONS TO EASE THE CURVE OF A SPINE, WALLS; THE SHOWPIECE OF ICONS, IDOLS, ANIMALS, EROTICA.

WHAT WAS THE LAST CONVERSATION?

SYLVIA GRANT

Whalley Range

Albert Square

Maine Road

Stanley Close

I REMEMBER BEFORE A DANCE IN THE LONG MIRROR WHEN ANN HAD SET MY HAIR, HAD SOMEONE'S OLD SUIT, COSTUME TAKEN IN, A SMALL WAIST, A FRILL, LOOKING OLDER TALLER AND WITH PLUCKED EYEBROWS NOT SO CLEAN-LOOKING!. "ROSY, FORWARD, YOU SHOULD WEAR PINK, IT'LL MATCH YOUR CHEEK". MY CHEEKS WERE. AND LATER THOSE DAMP CHIPS, THE SLOW WALK PAST THE PETROL STATION FOLLOWING THE BUS ROUTE. IT FELT LIKE SATURDAY NIGHT WAS KIND OF ON LOAN. AS THOSE DAYS THAT GO FROM COMMUNION TO CONFESSION. "LILY MARLENE", THE NEXT SAID, "WHERE DO YOUR LEGS END?" BEFORE SUNDAY.

Princess Road

Moss Side

Belle Vue

Exmouth Road

Southern Cemetery

Colour Supplements

PAUL CAPLIN

So where are they then?

You buy a photography book. You open it and what are you given? Words! Page after page of text. There are books with text, but never books with just pictures. Look at this for instance. I bought this book for Tynan's work, not for a commentary on it...

For Michel Foucault, the modern critic is a commentator, a parasite on contemporary culture. With intellectuals as commentators, Foucault argued, our culture is overrun with words and with commentary, becoming part of a post-modern condition where art and criticism merge into a mediascape of simulation, commentary and discourse.

...Just look at those 'arts' programmes on TV. They do these features on photography. The camera pans across the image, taking you on a guided tour while a 'critic' discusses, contextualises, comments, analyses... talks! Words, words everywhere, we never get to see pictures. They never get space. All we get are illustrations tagged on. They always follow the commentator, forced to be just supplements to a louder and prouder 'talk'...

For Jacques Derrida, Western culture has always been built around hierarchies, the privileging of one thing over another: serious discourse over non-serious, speech over writing. For Derrida, the creation of a 'supplement' is vital to our ways of seeing the world.

...I mean take the weekend colour magazines. Pictures squeezed into the space between futon ads, lingerie offers, lifestyles, 'the look' and last-minute flights. I want pictures, not reviews of books of exhibitions of pictures. I want images, full, clear without the cut-out coupon offering me a visual soundbite T-shirt. You can't find pictures nowadays. All you can find are substitutions for them.

For Jean Baudrillard, we live in an over-mediated world where media refer to media not reality, where images of images of images swamp our culture. No longer able to distinguish between fantasy and reality, we live in a perpetual Disneyland where art and kitsch slide into each other...

...Look at those 'meeja' courses: a module on TV, a module on Mills & Boon and a module on pho-

tography. There are no standards, just potentialities. Perm any three from five for a degree, a place on the TV circuit and position from which to add to the endless chatter of criticism. These cultural progressionals seem to think that judgement as to whether a photograph is good or not comes down to context, how it fits into a wider set of texts. It's just a picture, no more nor less important, truthful or powerful than any other media snatch...

For Richard Rorty, we can no longer do philosophy. In Baudrillard's media squared world we can no longer make judgements. What is true or good is what counts as true or good in a particular cultural setting. We exist in a set of language games where philosophy and politics are judged on how well they perform, and photography and pornography are merely two players in the endless dance of discourse.

...OK! Enough already! If we must have an intro-duction, a 'B-feature' to the main picture, let's get on with it. Tell us where and when he was born... Where did he study?... Oh, and most importantly, what camera does he use?... Tell us how you first 'came across his work'... What about an amusing anecdote? So important to get a rounded view of him... and you too of course! How about endless word pictures of a struggling young photographer fighting to get his work published in the face of the blizzard that is the Arts Council. What about a few paragraphs on his motivations. Is it true he was once locked under the stairs and found his Uncle Fester's battered Brownie?... All sorts of possibilities for a bit of analysis there. Oh his collar size would be useful! It does so help to get a picture of him rather than pictures by him...

For 'neo-pragmatists' like Rorty, photography can no longer have a critical edge. In a surface world, there is no danger, only talk of danger. There is no photography once photographic games. There is no criticism, only the dance of commentary. To talk of Tynan's work doing anything, is pointless. His images languish here alongside these words, a testament to a forgotten age when photographers spoke, critics spoke, politicians made statements not soundbites... and you could go to the pictures, have a packet of chips, and still have enough money for...

A golden age...

...Great! So why bother? I can't hope to reach Tynan's work, let alone get anything from it. I'll just be left wandering aimlessly through the virtual sprawl of this commentary, bemoaning the death of photography. Baudrillard and Rorty are right. There is no accessible reality, no truth-telling possibilities, merely games to be played. Foucault and Derrida are right. Wherever the photographer and her critic stand, they will always merely comment. Their work will always be supplementary to another more basic, more fundamental form. This work continually spins back on itself. Pictures and commentary dance around, suffocating whatever power either may have. The shout of words drowns out the pictures. The visual immediacy of the images dazzles the reader. Tynan's photographs are merely a supplement to my text...All is safe...All is play. There is no danger, no threat to the new world order.

"Robber" is dangerous however: a supplement but a dangerous one. Tynan's work, not just his images, but his practices, pull the rug from under hierarchical accounts of photography and criticism. In a state of colour supplements, "Robber" quietly, honestly undermines. Like the young boy at the parade, "Robber" nudges and points at the Emperor. Like the Sex Pistols on the Johnny Carson show, "Robber" punctuates consensus. Like a second voice, "Robber" whispers the unthinkable.

For Derrida, hierarchies are unstable. When our culture privileges speech over writing, claiming that the former is more immediate and more truthful, Derrida shows that the very attributes of writing, that we look down on (that because it uses symbols, it can equally well tell truths and untruths) is the very basis of a speech that also depends on flexible and adaptable formal symbols.

...In a culture where 'decisive moment' reportage and photographer as 'observer' still hold prominence, naturalism and realism take precedence over artifice and fantasy. The privileged work is the work of the instant, the captured moment. The privileged composition is the chance structure, the fleeting arrangement. The privileged mode is the transparent record... "Robber" undermines the privileging of photographic naturalism. By bringing the photographer, his intervention and his vision to the forefront, "Robber" quietly states that artifice, staging and power are at the heart of all photography. No matter how well the Leica is camouflaged, no matter how small the photographer makes herself, she is working within 'the photographic relationship', a magical relationship dependent on artifice and on power. The world of "Robber" is magical realist.

Magical realist writing uses fantasy to illuminate the problems literature has in dealing with the real. By building magic and fantasy into the narrative, writers such as Marquez, Allende, Rushdie and Winterson show the problems, politics and power at the heart of all representation.

In a global village built by an arts industry, photography is seen as a supplement to a more direct and analytical connection with the real. Analysis is privileged over-representation as surely as the preface pre-faces its object. Representation is marginalised as partial and ideological. "Robber" again

undermines such hierarchies. Tynan's world may be magical but his very presence in the work underpins the magic with a tense reality, a problematic relationship between Tynan, the person and their world. "Robber" proudly states "representation". It is built around ideology and power. As such, it forces the reader to engage with the ethics, politics and responsibilities of any form of representation, be it photographic or philosophic. Before she knows it, the reader is forced to see the problems of power and politics at the heart of any cultural project, not just the marginalised pictorial form. "Robber" is not secondary

to criticism. All criticism is a form of robbery...

..."Robber" also undermines the privileged status of portrait photography where the active subject of a portrait is privileged over the passive object of the paparazzi. The people in "Robber" are objects. They are the objects of Tynan's gaze, but it is their status as objects that enable them to speak, to achieve a subject position where they can quietly whisper "this is the nature of all photography...the portraitist has no clothes". Within the game that is "Robber", the people are not active subjects, their status slips through our fingers, undermining our attempts to position them...

Hypertext and hypermedia systems allow the 'author' to create an 'environment' where the 'reader' builds links and actively constructs the text. Rather than a hierarchy of author-subject and reader-object, hyper-environments generate reader-authors whose status and power slips out of our grasp as soon as we try to position it.

..."Robber" does more than start to undermine the naturalist-artist, criticism-representation and subject-object hierarchies in our culture. Tynan's work dangerously plays with the very status of the photographer. Whether the photographic culture privileges the observer over the artist, or whether the broader culture privileges the intellectual over the mere commentator-photographer, "Robber" undoes the very logic of those privileges. The photographer in "Robber" has come out of the Darkroom. Carrying lights, tripods and a neon camera, he proudly admits to his power position, challenging those in white coats or camouflage jackets to wake to the 'photographic relationship'. The photographer in "Robber" makes his statements, scuffed with involvement and soiled with power, showing up science for what it is: a power-full vision.

For Foucault, there is hope for the critic. She should take on the role of a 'specific intellectual'. Rather than making grandiose truth claims or an endless chain of commentary, she should place her own status as player on the line and speak from that position.

...It is tricks and breaks that are at the heart of "Robber". Just when we feel secure with an art book, documentary undermines. Just when we are comfortable reading a social document, artifice appears. Just when we see subjects, objects appear. Just when we read objects, the Subject appears. When we are secure in passivity, activity pulls the rug away. At every turn privileges and oppositions, stable positions for photographer, critic and reader are upset...

Wait a minute! The roles have been reversed. Who's speaking here? Who's providing the commentary now? Which is the main text? Whose is the dissident voice? Which is the real preface and which is the interloper? Which is foreground and which is background? Who is responding to whom?...

...It is time that the privileges separating preface and pictures are undermined. It is time that supplementary introductions become as dangerous as Tynan's lethal games with photography. It is time the form of the photographer's supplementary work appears as the basis of introductory games. It is time the content of the supplementary preface is seen as the basis of the photographer's statements.

...Fine, but all we're left with is games. You're spinning these pictures, your philosophers and me into just another corner of the media-scape where we'll endlessly refer to each other. Far from setting "Robber" apart from an all encompassing postmodern condition, you're spinning it into a quagmire of language games, commentary and an anaesthetized Disneyland of images and simulation. You've joined the ranks of the politically lobotomized. You might as well write 'coffee-table book' (or do I mean 'textbook') across the front and have done with it. There's more to Life than games...

..."Robber" operates as a text. In a world replete with texts, it operates as a dangerous supplement. Its uncompromising position on photography, power and representation shouts clearly that images and imaging can never be apolitical or outside power. Photo-books, catalogues and monographs are marginalised in our culture as picture interludes, as elements in a surface three-minute culture devoid of meaning, analysis, politics or statement. "Robber" refuses that position. Just as surely "Robber" refuses to take its place as a textbook. It has too many voices to make good rhetoric. It is too dialectical.

"Robber" is right. This work is criminal. It makes an unreasonable racket in a built-up culture. It drives on without due care and deference. It breaks and enters carefully built citadels. Above all, it is a breach of the peace...

Now do we get to see the other pictures?...

Mancunian Way

Old Trafford

Soap Works

"WE LIVED BACK TO BACK THEN". BONE TO BONE. "LOTS OF BROWN PAINT AROUND AND STRUGGLE, BUT HE COULD TURN MY TROUBLES AROUND, LIKE HE DID HIS SEEDLINGS, TO THE LIGHT".

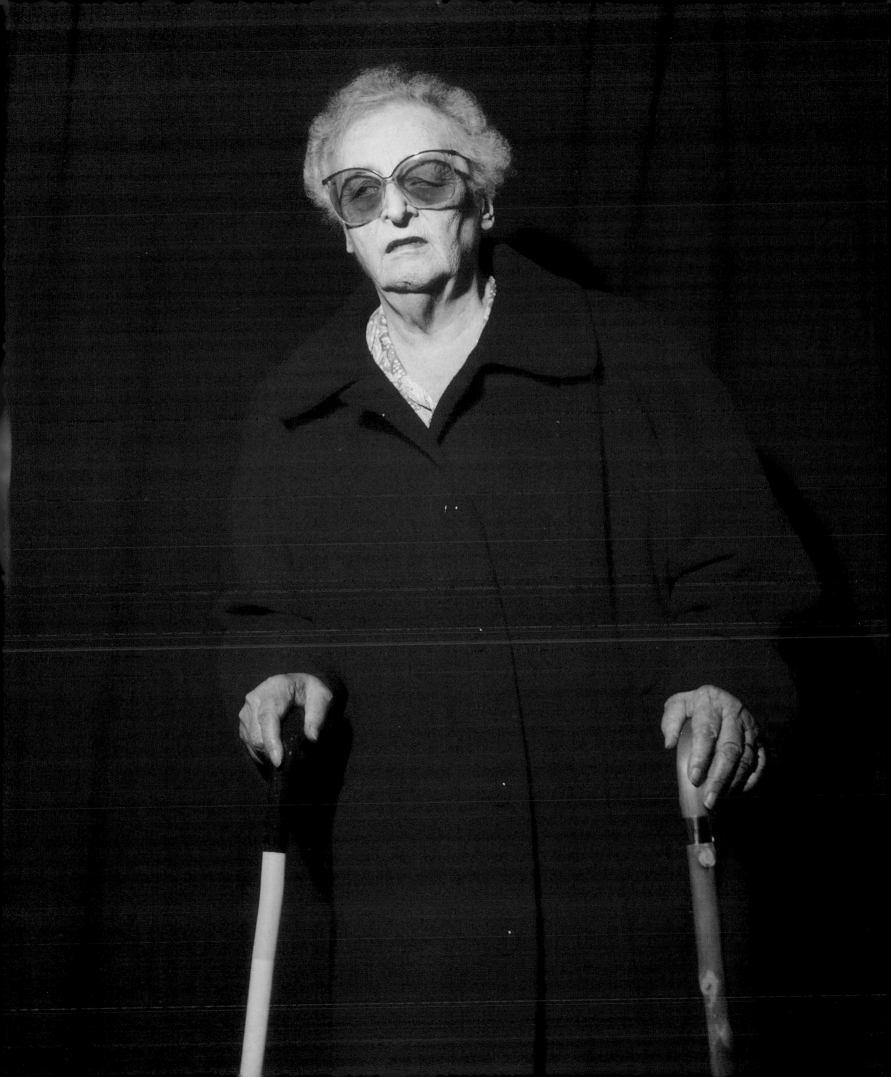

Recreation Ground

ACKNOWLEDGEMENTS

Of the many people who have given time to the production of this book, I would like especially to thank the following:

Lesley Stenson for her love and support, Mark Tynan for always being there, Sylvia Grant and Paul Caplin for their thought-provoking analysis of the work, Alan Ward for his design and enthusiasm for the project, Open Eye Gallery, David Williams, David Jaques, Catriona Henderson, North West Arts, Tony Woof, Ronnie Simpson, Michael Collins, John Holden, Alison Crosby, Cornerhouse Publications, David Tynan, Allison Hughes, David Glackin, Paul Duke, Mervyn Arthur, Daisy and Rosie, The Rumbergers, The Pilkington Centre St. Helens, for their patience and time.

I am most grateful for the generosity and enthusiasm shown to me by the many people who let me into their lives, for a brief period, so I could benefit and make this work.

STEVEN TYNAN